An Illustrated Guide

Mythical Creatures

A brief introduction to the varied life-forms of hearsay found in the myths, legends and folklore of cultures around the world, with illustrations by David West and text by Anita Ganeri.

Published in 2009 by

David West 👥 **Children's Books**
7 Princeton Court
55 Felsham Road
London SW15 1AZ

Copyright © 2009 David West Children's Books

First edition 2009

11 10 09
10 9 8 7 6 5 4 3 2 1

ISBN: 978 0 9553477 4 0

Designed and illustrated by David West
Written by Anita Ganeri and David West

A CIP catalogue record for this book is available from the British Library.

Photo Credits:
12tr, Hector Joseph Lumang; 12bl, Lynn Watson; 43ml, Sander Kamp; 43br, David Evans

Printed and bound in China.

Contents

Dragons, Serpents & Worms
—6—

Flying Creatures
—10—

Chimera
—17—

Half-Human, Half-Beast
—22—

Water Beasts
—28—

Giants
—32—

Shapeshifters
—38—

Demons, Ghouls & Ghosts
—42—

Glossary
—46—

Index
—48—

Introduction

Herein lies a magical world of strange creatures and fabulous beasts, where the Cockatrice's glance can turn a person to stone, and the trumpet of the Manticore lures unsuspecting travellers to their doom. Here be knights riding Hippogriffs, heroes battling dragons, Scorpion men guarding the tombs of the dead, and giants fighting gods.

Dare to turn the pages of this book to discover a world of myth and legend brought to life in beautiful colour illustrations.

A knight battles a dragon to rescue a maiden.

Dragons, Serpents & Worms

Here be dragons...Dragons appear in almost every mythology around the world, as immense, lizard-like beasts covered in scales. They hatch from eggs after thousands of years, and are sometimes said to spit poison or breathe fire.

Y Ddraig Gosh, the Welsh red dragon

Dragons East and West

As with most creatures of myth, dragons are understood and depicted in different ways by different cultures. Eastern dragons – most notably from China and Japan – are very powerful but usually benevolent. They are revered for their great wisdom, and are often worshipped as mythical rulers of nature and the weather, particularly of water and rain. Unlike Western dragons, these dragons do not have wings because it is believed that they fly by magic.

In the mythologies of the West, most dragons are dangerous. Some live in caves where they fiercely guard hoards of gold and treasure. Others terrorise towns and villages, demanding human sacrifices to eat. Unlike Eastern dragons, there are numerous legends of these terrible beasts being hunted down and killed. Dragon slayers are famous and heroic characters in Western folklore. In Greek mythology, Prince Cadmus is sent in search of his missing sister, Europa. He fails to find her but decides to found a city on a spot guarded by a serpent-like dragon, which he kills. In medieval times, there were many famous dragon slayers like Siegfried, hero of the German Niebelungenlied. He kills the dragon, Fafnir, and drinks its blood. This makes him invulnerable, apart from one small spot on his shoulder.

In Eastern mythology, the Azure Dragon is one of the four symbols of the constellation. It represents the East, spring and the element of wood.

One of the most famous dragon slayers of Christian folklore is St George, shown in the 15th-century Russian icon above. Legend says that he killed a dragon which was about to devour the king's daughter.

Eastern dragons, like the one in this Japanese dragon shrine, are often shown with a large pearl in their grasp, though some say that it is really the dragon's egg.

Wyverns and Lindworms

Although it has similarities to a European dragon, the legendary Wyvern differs in having only two legs, with large wings instead of front limbs, and sometimes with eagle's claws on the tips. It is unsure whether Wyverns breathe fire, like dragons, but they have deadly arrow-shaped barbs at the ends of their tails for killing their prey. In medieval Europe, Wyverns were associated with war, pestilence and plague. Their images are seen today as heraldic emblems on coats of arms, crests and flags. Here, they are usually seen as a symbol of strength and endurance. Wyverns are closely related to Lindworms which appear in Scandinavian and German mythology. Lindworms are often described as having the body of a serpent with a poisonous bite. These enormous and terrifying beasts eat cattle, and are believed to raid churchyards to devour the dead.

Since 1730, the Zilant, a Wyvern, has been the official emblem of Kazan, Russia.

Wyverns are said to be more aggressive than dragons and to prey on humans and livestock.

Worms

In northern European mythology, the word for dragon is 'worm' which means snake or serpent. In old English, it is 'wyrm'. Legends from the Middle Ages describe Worms as serpents with no wings or legs but with dragons' heads. One of the best-known stories is the tale of the Lambton Worm. It tells how a young man, called John Lambton, catches a Worm while out fishing in the local river, and throws it down a nearby well. Over the years, the beast grows to a huge size and attacks the local livestock and villagers. Many knights are killed as they attempt to slay the beast. Finally, John Lambton succeeds in killing the Worm but his family fall under a terrible curse as a result.

Lambton fights the Worm by the river so that the water carries away the pieces of the beast before they can join up to form its body again.

Feathered Serpent

For thousands of years, Quetzalcoatl, the feathered serpent, was one of the most important characters in Aztec mythology, religion and art. Often depicted as a snake with a headdress made from quetzal bird feathers, Quetzalcoatl was also the wind god, the patron god of priests and responsible for the creation of the world.

Quetzalcoatl devouring a man from the Codex Telleriano-Remensis.

Many-headed Serpents

In Ancient Greek legend, the hero, Heracles, is set the task of killing the Hydra, a huge snake with numerous heads, and breath so poisonous it can kill human beings. On reaching Lake Lerna, Heracles fires burning arrows into the Hydra's lair to draw out the monstrous beast. But each time Heracles cuts off one of its heads, two more heads grow in its place. Heracles calls on his nephew, Ioalus, for help. After each head is cut off, Ioalus seals the stump with a burning branch until, at last, the Hydra is dead. In a later task, Heracles also kills the hundred-headed serpent, Ladon, which guards the Garden of Hesperides, in order to steal the apples of immortality.

The Garden of Hesperides, painted by Frederic Leighton.

Heracles battles with the Hydra, a many-headed serpent.

Giant Serpents

Many cultures have myths describing giant serpents that do battle with the gods. These conflicts often represent the struggle of good versus evil, as in the Ancient Egyptian myth of Apep. Apep is a giant serpent that embodies all that is evil. He represents darkness and chaos and is, therefore, the arch enemy of order and light. Every night, as the Sun god, Ra, sinks below the horizon, he does battle with Apep in the underworld but always returns victorious in the morning to the sky.

In Norse mythology, Jormungandr, the serpent, is so enormous that he can circle Midgard (the world of humans) under the ocean and hold his own tail in his mouth. He is greatly feared by sailors who venture into the deep waters where he lives. Jormungandr's arch enemy is Thor, the god of thunder. One story tells how Thor goes fishing with the giant, Hymir. As Thor rows further out to sea, Hymir warns him that they are in danger. Thor ignores the giant's warning and casts his line, baited with an ox's head, which Jormungandr snatches. After a great struggle, Thor pulls the serpent from the water, and is about to kill him when Hymir cuts the line and it escapes. Thor and Jormundgandr are destined to meet again at Ragnarok (the final battle), when Thor will kill the serpent only to fall dead himself from Jormungandr's poison.

A painting of Thor fighting the Midgard serpent, by Henry Fuseli.

An Ancient Egyptian painting showing a god warding off the serpent, Apep.

Roger rides a Hippogriff to rescue Angelique.

Flying Creatures

Folk tales, myths, legends and heraldry are filled with examples of fantastical flying creatures and winged beasts.

None is more majestic that the fabulous Griffin, with the body of a lion, and the head and wings of an eagle.

An illustration of a Griffin by Sir John Tenniel for Lewis Carroll's Alice in Wonderland

A Peryton

The Simurgh

Part Bird...

Tales of Griffins reached Europe from ancient Scythia where these legendary beasts were said to line their nests with gold, killing anyone who dared steal it from them. In medieval times, it was believed that a Griffin's feathers and claws had magical powers. The feathers were thought to cure blindness. A cup made from a griffin claw could warn of the presence of poison by changing colour. Rarer still than the Griffin was the Hippogriff, the offspring of a Griffin and a horse. Hippogriffs were extremely rare because Griffins and horses were arch enemies.

Another mythical bird-like beast was the Peryton which had the forelegs, head, and antlers of a stag, and the wings, feathers and back legs of a bird. Said to come from the legendary land of Atlantis, the Peryton cast the shadow of a man.

In Persian mythology, the Simurgh is a bird with a dog's head and lion's claws. Its wings are so huge that they could block out the sun. It is said to have lived for so long that it is the keeper of all knowledge.

One of the most famous flying creatures of all is Pegasus, the winged horse of ancient Greek mythology who carries the hero, Bellerophon, to kill the Chimera (see page 17). A similar winged horse, known as Buraq, appears in Islamic literature and art.

Buraq from a 17th-century Mughal miniature

Pegasus and Bellerophon

Other winged creatures

The Hsigo, or Hsaio, is a monkey with wings that appears in Chinese folklore. Its presence is believed to warn of serious drought. The legend of the Hsigo may have inspired the flying monkeys in the book 'The Wonderful Wizard of Oz'. Human-headed lions and bulls, called Shedu or Lamassu, come from Ancient Assyria. Sculptures of these creatures were placed as guardians at the entrances of cities and palaces.

Hsigos in flight

Harpies and Sirens

Bird-like creatures with human heads appear in mythology throughout the world. Among the most terrible are the Harpies of Ancient Greece. They torment humans by stealing their food and screeching so that their victims cannot eat or rest. It was said that the only thing they were frightened of was the sound made by a brass instrument.

Sirens look similar to Harpies but Greek stories tell how they used their beautiful singing voice to lure sailors to their deaths on the rocks. In Russian mythology, they were known as Sirins, and were equally dangerous. Humans who heard their song forgot everything else to follow them, ultimately to their death.

Sirin (left) and Alkonost, birds of joy and sorrow, by Vicktor Vasnetsov (1896)

A sculpture of a Lamassu from Ancient Assyria

In this 1891 painting by John William Waterhouse, the Greek hero, Odysseus, tied to the mast, survives the Sirens' song. On the advice of an enchantress, he blocks the ears of his men with bees' wax so that they cannot hear their fateful music.

Giant Birds

The Roc was an enormous mythical bird so strong that it was believed to be able to carry off and eat elephants. From the Middle East, the legend of the Roc reached the West through Marco Polo's account of his travels, and The 1001 Nights which included the story of Sinbad the Sailor. In reality, the Roc may have been inspired by the elephant bird of Madagascar which became extinct in the 16th century.

In The 1001 Nights, Sinbad the Sailor's ship is destroyed by a Roc.

Other giant birds of legend include Vucub-Cacquix ('Seven Macaw'), the Mayan giant bird-demon which claimed to be the Sun and the Moon; the Chinese Peng which could fly for six months without resting; and the Ziz from Jewish mythology, which had wings that could block out the sun.

A Phoenix painted on the walls of a tower used for burnt offerings in Tian Hou Temple, Shenzhen, Guangdon, China.

Fire and Thunder Birds

In Native North American legend, the Thunderbird is a mythical bird of immense power and strength. It is believed that the beating of its huge wings causes the sound of thunder and that lightning flashes from its eyes. Similarly, the South African Impundulu, or 'lightning bird', is a black and white bird, the size of a human, which summons thunder and lightning with its wings and claws.

Perhaps the most famous firebird is the fabulous Phoenix of Ancient Egyptian, Phoenician and later myths. There is only one Phoenix at a time, although it lives for hundreds of years. At the end of its life, it builds a nest of sweet-smelling twigs. Both the nest and bird burn to ashes, from which a new, young Phoenix arises.

In Russian mythology, the Firebird is a large bird with glowing feathers. Finding a lost feather inspires many heroes to set out to find and capture a live bird. These quests traditionally cause the hero great hardship for which he blames the Firebird.

Images of the Thunderbird are popular in Native North American art and often appear carved on totem poles.

Prince Ivan returns from his quest on a magic carpet with a caged Firebird, by Viktor Vasnetsov.

Eros

Since ancient times, human beings or human-like creatures with wings have featured in the world's myths and legends. In Greek mythology, Eros is sometimes said to be the son of Ares, god of war, and Aphrodite, goddess of beauty. He is a charming but mischievous god who specialises in making people fall in love by piercing them with his golden arrows. He himself falls in love with a beautiful woman, called Psyche, when he grazes himself on one of his own arrows. In Roman mythology, Eros becomes Cupid. He is usually shown as a young boy, or sometimes a child, with his bow and arrows in hand.

Hermes

Eros had two kinds of arrows. His golden arrows with dove feathers caused people to fall in love instantly. His lead arrows with owl feathers led to disinterest.

Messengers of the Gods

Hermes is the Greek god who acts as a messenger between the gods of Mount Olympus and human beings. He is given the task by Apollo, to keep him out of trouble. He is shown wearing winged sandals and a winged helmet to speed his flight between the worlds of the mortals and immortals. Hermes is also the protector of travellers and thieves. In Roman mythology, the equivalent deity is Mercury.

Garuda

In Hindu mythology, Garuda is usually shown with the body of a man but the wings and beak of an eagle. He is the king of the birds, often chosen to carry the great god, Vishnu, and the enemy of snakes and Nagas (see page 24). Garuda's story is told in the great Hindu sacred text, The Mahabharata, in which he is a symbol of speed and military strength. Huge birds, called Garudas, also appear in Buddhist mythology. They are said to create hurricane-force winds when they flap their gigantic wings.

Worshipping Garuda is believed to cleanse the body of poisons.

14

Angels

Angels are supernatural beings found in many religions. In Christianity, Islam and Judaism, they are heavenly beings, created by God, who are sent down to Earth to instruct people about God's wishes or to perform other tasks. While angels are generally agreed to be invisible to human sight, they are often shown as human-like creatures with varying pairs of wings. In Islamic belief, angels are made by Allah (God) from light but can take on any form they choose, human or otherwise. They are neither male nor female, and are immortal.

In the 17th-century painting by Guido Reni, the archangel Michael is shown in military dress as he fights against Satan.

Tengus

Tengus are spirit-like creatures which appear in Japanese folklore in many different forms. They are usually shown with both bird-like and human characteristics, including a bright red face and extremely long nose. Tengus take their name from a fierce dog-like demon in Chinese mythology which brought war and caused thunder. In early Japanese stories, they were enemies of Buddhism, kidnapping monks and robbing temples. They later returned their victims, in a state of madness or near-death. In later tales, Tengus are divided into good and bad spirits. Some religious groups worshipped them as gods who protected sacred mountains and forests. In popular folk stories, Tengus are often portrayed as comical creatures who are easily tricked by humans. In one tale, a boy tricks a Tengu into exchanging its magic cloak of invisibility for a humble piece of bamboo.

A 19th-century woodprint by Utagawa Kuniyoshi, showing an elephant catching a flying Tengu.

A Leyak

Flying Heads

In the mythology of Bali, Leyaks are hideous flying creatures that haunt graveyards and feed on dead bodies. By day, they appear as ordinary humans. At night, their gruesome heads and entrails break out of their bodies and fly.

15

One look from the Cockatrice can turn a person to stone.

Chimera

Chimera are creatures made of the parts of different animals. The name comes from the Chimera of Greek mythology, a fire-breathing beast with the head of a lion, the body of a huge goat and the tail of a serpent.

The Chimera's father was Typhon, god of the wind, and its mother Echidna, a monster who was part-woman, part-snake. It is eventually killed by the hero, Bellerophon, riding Pegasus, the winged horse (see page 11).

Mixed up Creatures

Mythologies around the world have thrown up bizarre and outlandish Chimera. The Ahuizotl of Aztec myth is an extraordinary creature that is half-dog, half-monkey with a human hand protruding from the end of its tail. It was believed to live near water and snatches people who venture too close to the water's edge, or fishermen in their boats. The Ahuizotl is greatly feared because of its fondness for eating human flesh.

In Japanese mythology, a Nue is a beast with a monkey's head, a raccoon dog's body, a tiger's legs and a snake for a tail. It is said that a Nue can change itself into a black cloud and fly, bringing bad luck and illness.

One of the most feared Chimera is the Cockatrice. This dreaded creature resembles a large cockerel, with dragon's wings and a serpent's tail. It was originally linked to another beast, called a Basilisk, although the Basilisk always takes snake form. The Cockatrice's magic powers include a deadly stare that can kill people or turn them to stone. It can only be killed if its stare is reflected back at it from a polished surface, such as a mirror, or if it hears a cockerel crow. The weasel, the Cockatrice's arch enemy, is the only animal that can survive its gaze.

A stone plaque dating from around 1500 from a temple at Tepoztlan, south of Mexico City, which shows the Ahuizotl.

A woodprint from 1852 showing a Nue, disguised as a black cloud, descending on the royal palace.

A woodblock print of a Basilisk from 1642

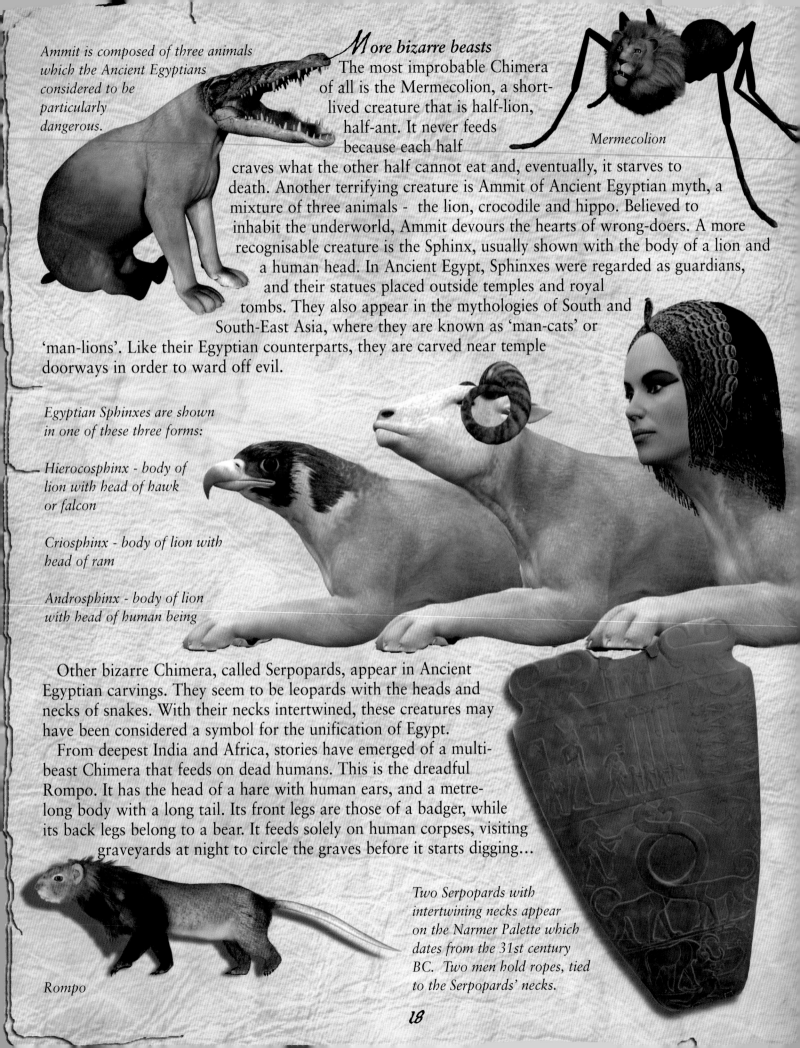

Ammit is composed of three animals which the Ancient Egyptians considered to be particularly dangerous.

More bizarre beasts

The most improbable Chimera of all is the Mermecolion, a short-lived creature that is half-lion, half-ant. It never feeds because each half craves what the other half cannot eat and, eventually, it starves to death. Another terrifying creature is Ammit of Ancient Egyptian myth, a mixture of three animals - the lion, crocodile and hippo. Believed to inhabit the underworld, Ammit devours the hearts of wrong-doers. A more recognisable creature is the Sphinx, usually shown with the body of a lion and a human head. In Ancient Egypt, Sphinxes were regarded as guardians, and their statues placed outside temples and royal tombs. They also appear in the mythologies of South and South-East Asia, where they are known as 'man-cats' or 'man-lions'. Like their Egyptian counterparts, they are carved near temple doorways in order to ward off evil.

Mermecolion

Egyptian Sphinxes are shown in one of these three forms:

Hierocosphinx - body of lion with head of hawk or falcon

Criosphinx - body of lion with head of ram

Androsphinx - body of lion with head of human being

Other bizarre Chimera, called Serpopards, appear in Ancient Egyptian carvings. They seem to be leopards with the heads and necks of snakes. With their necks intertwined, these creatures may have been considered a symbol for the unification of Egypt.

From deepest India and Africa, stories have emerged of a multi-beast Chimera that feeds on dead humans. This is the dreadful Rompo. It has the head of a hare with human ears, and a metre-long body with a long tail. Its front legs are those of a badger, while its back legs belong to a bear. It feeds solely on human corpses, visiting graveyards at night to circle the graves before it starts digging…

Rompo

Two Serpopards with intertwining necks appear on the Narmer Palette which dates from the 31st century BC. Two men hold ropes, tied to the Serpopards' necks.

Heraldic Beasts

Many weird and wonderful Chimera have appeared as heraldic symbols on crests and shields. These beasts have specific meanings - lions represent strength and courage; horses are symbols of readiness for duty. Animals are combined to give greater significance. An Alphyn has a lion's head and body, with an eagle's claws and a long tongue. The Calygreyhound symbolises swiftness. It is said to have the body of a deer, the front legs of an eagle, the back legs and hooves of an ox, and the head of a wild cat. Another heraldic beast is the Enfield which has the head of a fox, a greyhound's chest, a lion's body, the back legs and tail of a wolf, and eagle's claws on its front legs. It is said to possess the qualities of each of these animals, for example, a fox's cunning.

The legendary Ypotryll is a heraldic Chimera with a boar's head and tusks, a camel's humped body, the legs of a goat or ox, and a serpent's tail.

Alphyn

Calygreyhound

Enfield

The Questing Beast

In Arthurian legend, the Questing Beast is a strange creature that many brave knights 'quest', or attempt to hunt. The beast is sometimes said to resemble a leopard, with a serpent's head and neck, a lion's tail and back legs, and a deer's hooves. In other texts, however, it is described as being a small creature and pure white in colour.

Some knights dedicated their lives to their search for the Questing Beast.

The Good

Most mythical creatures seem to have been born out of human fears. A few, however, break this mould and tend towards the side of good. The Unicorn of Western myth is one such legendary beast. Popularly, a Unicorn was seen as a beautiful white or grey horse-like creature with a single, spiral horn growing from its forehead. In fact it was a Chimera made up of a horse, with a goat's cloven hooves and a lion's tail. It was thought to be a magical beast and to have healing powers. In addition, its horn can detect poison in food and drink, then purify it and make them safe to eat and drink. Its horn was so valuable that the Unicorn was hunted to extinction, it is said. Although the Unicorn was a wild and formidable creature, hunters knew a way of catching it. A maiden was used to enchant it so that it fell asleep in her lap. Then the hunters cut off its horn.

It was said that only a gentle and pure maiden had the power to tame a Unicorn.

The Qilin from Chinese mythology is sometimes called the 'Chinese Unicorn' but it differs greatly in appearance (see right) and character. Despite its fearsome looks, it is considered to be a good omen, heralding peace or prosperity. It is so gentle that it can walk on grass but not trample it or harm any insects, and so peaceful that its diet does not include meat. Even so, it can become fierce and breathe fire if it sees a wicked person threaten a good, pure person. In Japanese legend, the Qilin is called a Kirin. It looks more like a Western Unicorn than a Qilin does but its body is covered in scales.

A Japanese woodprint showing a Baku.

Japanese mythology also has the Baku, another beneficial Chimera. It has been described in many different ways, combining parts of the bodies of elephants, rhinos and tigers. The Baku has long appeared in Japanese folk tales as a creature which devours, and thus prevents, people's nightmares.

Part-dragon, part-deer, and part-ox, the Chinese Qilin is also covered in scales.

The Bad...

Probably one of the scariest Chimeras is the Manticore. This legendary creature has the body of a lion, and the head of a human, with three rows of savage, sharp teeth. It has the tail of a dragon or serpent which can shoot out poisonous spines or hairs to paralyse prey. This terrible beast is said to range in size from lion-sized to horse-sized. The Manticore originated in Persian mythology, where its name meant 'man-eater'. It is thought to kill its victims instantly with a bite or scratch, then to eat all of them, including their bones.

Tales of Manticores are still told in parts of Asia. If a person disappears, it is believed that the Manticore has eaten them.

One kind of Ushi-oni is a huge, ferocious sea monster with the body of a crab and the head of a bull. It is said to live off the coast where it attacks fishermen.

The Ushi-oni is another terrifying Chimera which appears in Japanese folklore. There are various kinds of Ushi-oni, but all of them are monstrous with the horned heads of cattle. Tales are told of Ushi-oni who were persuaded to help farmers to plough their fields. They did the work amazingly fast but, of course, demanded their dues in the end...

The Tarasque was a fearsome monster that caused chaos and devastation across Provence, in France. Many knights tried and failed to capture it, until Saint Martha tamed it and led it back to the city where the people attacked it and it died.

The Tarasque was a bizarre-looking Chimera with a lion's head, six bear-like legs, an ox-like body covered with a turtle's shell, and a scaly tail with a scorpion's sting.

Catoblepas

...And the Ugly

From Ethiopia comes a Chimera, called a Catoblepas. It is said to resemble a black buffalo, with a pig's head which is so large and heavy, it always hangs down to the ground. Woe betide anyone who comes across a Catoblepas. Like the Basilisk (see page 17), its stare and breath are reputed to be fatal, killing people or turning them to stone.

21

Centaurs carrying off nymphs.

22

Half-human, half-beast

The famous Centaur, Chiron, was a wise teacher of Greek heroes, including Achilles.

Strange-looking creatures composed of unexpected combinations of animal and human parts have appeared throughout mythology since ancient times. They are shown as animals with human heads or torsos, or as humans with animal heads.

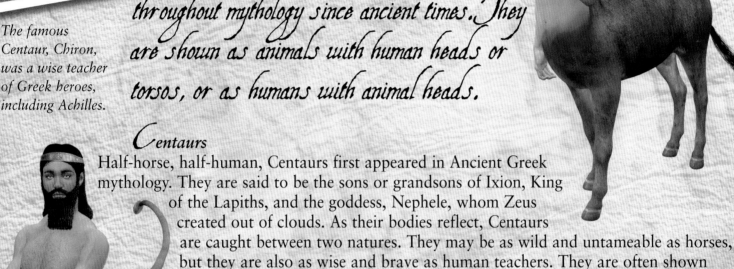

An Onocentaur, with the top half of a human and the body of a donkey

Centaurs

Half-horse, half-human, Centaurs first appeared in Ancient Greek mythology. They are said to be the sons or grandsons of Ixion, King of the Lapiths, and the goddess, Nephele, whom Zeus created out of clouds. As their bodies reflect, Centaurs are caught between two natures. They may be as wild and untameable as horses, but they are also as wise and brave as human teachers. They are often shown carrying off nymphs, when their wild side comes to the fore. Female Centaurs, called Kentaurides, appear in later Greek and Roman myths. Later still, there appears the Onocentaur, a creature with a human top half and a donkey's body.

Centaurs from Mesopotamia

Centaur-like creatures are also found in the ancient myths of Mesopotamia. The Urmahlullu, or 'lion-man', is a guardian spirit with the body of a lion and the head and torso of a human. Centaurs with lions' bodies also appear in English heraldry, for example in the emblems of the 12th-century King Stephen.

In Mesopotamia, statues of the Urmahlullu stood outside the rooms where the priests ritually washed.

Several Mesopotamian myths feature Centaurs with the bodies of scorpions. In the famous Epic of Gilgamesh, they stand guard outside the gates to the land of the Sun god, Shamash. They open the gates as the Sun god rises.

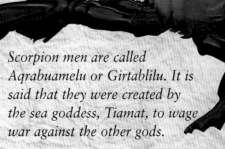

Scorpion men are called Aqrabuamelu or Girtablilu. It is said that they were created by the sea goddess, Tiamat, to wage war against the other gods.

Snake People

In Hindu mythology, Nagas are serpent gods that play an important part in religion. They often appear as beings that are half-human, half-snake, or as snakes with multiple heads, each one hooded like a cobra's. Nagas are linked with water, protecting wells and rivers, and controlling life-giving rainclouds. Hugely powerful, their only enemy is the giant bird-man, Garuda (see page 14). Tales about Nagas are also commonly found in Buddhist mythology, where a Naga, called Mucalinda, uses its hood to shelter the Buddha from a great storm. Chinese tales tell of Nuwa, a creature that is half-woman, half-snake. She is said to have created humans out of lumps of clay, and to have repaired the sky after a terrible catastrophe destroyed the world.

A female Naga is called a Nagini. Legend says that Nagas are dangerous to humans but only if they have been provoked or angered.

Nuwa and her husband Fuxi

Satyrs and Fauns

The Satyrs of Greek mythology are woodland creatures who are human down to the waist, apart from pointed ears and horns, but with a goat's hairy legs and hooves. They are the pleasure-loving followers of Pan, the god of shepherds and hunting, who is often shown playing pipes. Their favourite occupations are drinking wine and chasing nymphs. Their counterparts in Roman myths are known as Fauns.

A similar half-human creature from Greek legend is an Ipotane. Its name means 'horse-person' and it is shown as having a horse's hindquarters, legs and tail, with the head and upper body of a human.

An Ipotane

Pan is famous for his music. It inspires people or causes panic, depending on his intentions.

24

The Minotaur

The famous Minotaur of Greek mythology is a terrible monster with the body of a man and the head of a huge bull. His father is a white bull sent to King Minos of Crete by Poseidon, the sea god; his human mother, Pasiphae, is King Minos's wife. The Minotaur lives deep inside the maze-like Labyrinth, which Minos has built to contain him. After defeating Athens in war, Minos demands that the Athenian king send seven boys and seven girls every year to be devoured by the Minotaur. With the help of Minos's daughter, Ariadne, the hero, Theseus, finally succeeds in killing the Minotaur. He takes with him a ball of thread given to him by Ariadne so that he can follow it and find his way safely out of the Labyrinth again.

In Greek, Minotaur means 'Bull of Minos'. The historical site of Knossos in Crete is thought to be the site of the Labyrinth.

Animal-headed gods

Many cultures from around the world revere deities with animal heads. In the Hindu religion, Ganesha, the elephant-headed god, is one of the best-known and most honoured gods. He is believed to remove obstacles and is worshipped at the beginning of every new task. Most stories tell how Ganesha, the son of the goddess, Parvati, and the great god, Shiva, is born with a human head and body. Later, however, Shiva beheads him in a quarrel. Shiva then replaces Ganesha's original head with that of an elephant.

An ancient name for Ganesha is 'Ekadanta' or 'One-tusked'. This refers to the fact that he has only one whole tusk, the other having broken off.

In the mythology and religion of Ancient Egypt, many deities are portrayed with the heads of animals. Among them are Bastet, a mother goddess, with the head of a cat, and Sobek, the god of water, with the head of a crocodile.

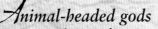

The Ancient Egyptian gods, Bastet and Sobek

Dog-headed

A dog-headed human is called a Cynocephalus. These creatures feature in many writings from medieval times. They are often used to depict people from far-distant lands who appeared outlandish to early explorers.

An illustration of a Cynocephalus from a 15th-century printed book

25

Man or Caiman

The legend of El Hombre Caiman, or the 'Caiman Man', comes from the north coast of Colombia in South America. He is said to have been a fisherman originally, who is enchanted by a river spirit and turned into a caiman. He returns to the river once a year to hunt for human victims to feed on.

El Hombre Caiman

Cow face

The Chichevache is a cow with a human face that appears in European mythology. It is said to prey on good wives but to be constantly starving due to the lack of women who have been faithful to their husbands. Whereas, it is said that the Bicorne, a type of two-horned Unicorn, is always fat and well fed because it only eats kind and obedient husbands, and they are in plentiful supply.

The Chichevache

Medusa

In Greek mythology, Medusa is one of three monstrous sisters, called the Gorgons. Originally a beautiful nymph, Medusa offends the goddess, Athene, who turns her flowing locks of hair into writhing snakes and makes her face so terrible that one glance can turn a person into stone. Medusa is eventually killed by the hero, Perseus, who looks at her reflection in his shield to guide him, then cuts her head off. Two beings spring from her blood - Pegasus, the winged horse (see page 11), and the giant, Chrysaor.

Perseus gives Medusa's head to Athene, to place on her shield for protection.

26

Fig: 3.

Vir marinus episcopi specie An 1531 captus in mari Baltico.

An engraving of a Merman, supposedly caught in the Baltic Sea in the 16th century.

A Mermaid has the head and upper body of a woman and the tail of a fish. Stories of Mermaids may have been based on sightings of sea animals, such as dolphins or manatees.

Mere Folk

Almost every culture has legends which tell of magical creatures that are half-human and half-fish. The image of a beautiful fish-tailed woman sitting on a rock has beguiled sailors for millennia. Stories of Mermaids date back at least as far as Ancient Assyria. A goddess called Atargatis, the mother of the queen, falls in love with a mortal shepherd and, by doing so, causes his death. Filled with remorse, she jumps into a lake and takes the form of a Mermaid.

Sighting a Mermaid was often unlucky and foretold disaster. Some tales tell how Mermaids, much like Sirens (see page 12), would sing to sailors, thus enchanting them and causing shipwrecks. They were also said to drag drowning men down into their undersea kingdoms. In some stories, they can only become immortal by marrying a human being. The less common, male equivalent of the Mermaid is the Merman. The most famous may be the Greek god, Triton, son of the sea god, Poseidon. He blows on a conch shell to calm or whip up the waves.

Similarly, fish-like people appear in many mythologies. The Rusalki of Russia are said to live at the bottom of rivers. The Jengu of Cameroon bring good luck and can cure disease. The Merrow of Ireland and Scotland wear magical caps that allow them to live underwater. The Melusine of European folklore are believed to be spirits of sacred rivers and streams. Like Mermaids, they have the body of a woman but are sometimes shown with wings and two tails. They appear in German heraldry with a tail draped over each arm, and sometimes wearing a crown. Medieval stories tell of Melusine marrying mortal men.

Other mythical water creatures include Selkies from Scotland who can transform themselves from seals into humans by removing their animal skins (see page 40).

The Ichthyocentaur, or fish centaur, was an extraordinary creature with a human body, a fish's tail and the front legs of a horse.

A Sea Monk is said to be a monstrous fish that looks like a monk.

A Kraken attacks sailors and their ship.

Water Beasts

Some of the largest creatures in mythology are water beasts, in particular those that live in the oceans. Reports from sailors, even today, tell of strange and fearsome monsters that attack them and their ships.

A boatful of unfortunate sailors land on the Aspidochelone's back.

Sea Serpents and other Monsters of the Deep

Sea serpents appear in many mythologies, especially those of maritime countries. Some people believe that they are actual sea creatures, such as whales or sharks, exaggerated in size and danger by frightened sailors. Others think that they might be the sole surviving examples of prehistoric sea reptiles. Whatever their origins, sea serpents are usually reported as being gigantic creatures.

The Aspidochelone, known from medieval texts, is supposed to have been the size of an island. In Norse mythology, Jormungandr (see page 9) is so long, its body can encircle the whole world. More recent sightings include a serpent some 20 metres long, sighted in 1848 by the crew of HMS Daedalus while on an Atlantic voyage.

The Leviathan is a Biblical sea monster whose name has come to mean any enormous, whale-like sea creature. In one legend the Leviathan is believed to devour one whale a day. Later reports state that it is able to swallow whole ships.

In his book, 'History of the Northern Peoples', 16th-century Swedish writer, Olaus Magnus, describes many sea monsters such as this serpent.

The Kraken

The legendary Kraken of Scandinavian mythology is another enormous sea monster, with immense tentacles. Sailors not only feared the monster itself but the powerful whirlpool it created when it suddenly descended into the sea. This could suck down even the biggest of ships. It may be that the story of the Kraken originated from sightings of giant squid.

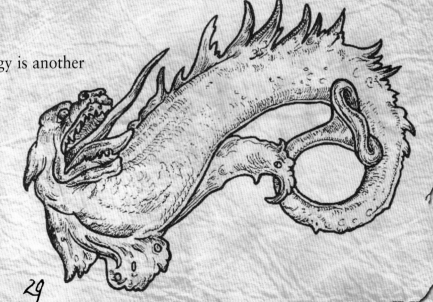

An artist's impression of the Biblical Leviathan

Scylla and Charybdis

In Greek mythology, Scylla and Charybdis are terrifying monsters that guard the two sides of a strait (channel of water). The channel is so narrow that it is impossible for sailors to navigate safely between the two. Scylla is a grotesque sea monster with six snapping heads and a ring of snarling dogs around her waist. Originally a sea nymph, Charybdis takes the form of a gigantic whirlpool that sucks ships down to their doom. According to Homer's Odyssey, the hero, Odysseus is one of the very few successfully to navigate the channel by sailing closer to Scylla, even though the monster kills six of his men.

When Scylla kills Odysseus's men, he takes the oars and helps to row the ship to safety through the strait.

Sea-horses and Sea-lions

Hippocampus is the Greek word for the tiny and unusual fish, known as sea horses in English. In Greek mythology, however, it is a huge creature with the body of a horse and the tail of a fish or dolphin that pulls the chariot of Poseidon, god of the sea. Fish-tailed creatures also appear in Etruscan legend. They include Leokampai (fish-tailed lions), Taurokampoi (fish-tailed bulls) and Pardalokampoi (fish-tailed leopards).

Leokampoi and Hippocampus

The Nuckelavee

The Nuckelavee

A terrible sea-monster, the Nuckelavee is found in Celtic mythology. This hideous creature has legs which are partly finned, and a horse's body with a human head and torso growing out of its back. Its enormous mouth gapes open, and its single eye burns with a red flame. More gruesomely still, the beast has no skin on its body. The Nuckelavee is said to live mainly in the sea but cannot cross running water, such as rivers and streams. It occasionally rampages across the land, spreading plague and causing crops to die.

Lake monsters

Over many centuries, there have been numerous stories of huge animals living in lakes across the world. Although frequently sighted, no specimens have ever been caught and the existence of these animals has not been proved. Perhaps the most famous lake monster is the Loch Ness Monster, said to inhabit Loch Ness in Scotland. Similar monsters have been widely reported in North America, such as Ogopogo in Okanagan Lake, Champ in Lake Champlain, and Manipogo in Lake Manitoba.

The Loch Ness Monster

Bunyips, Kappas and Kelpies

According to Australian aboriginal legend, the Bunyip, a large, fearsome devil, lurks in rivers, creeks, lakes and swamps. It is sometimes described as having a dog-like face, dark fur, a horse-like tail, flippers, and walrus-like tusks or horns. Its blood-curdling roar can be heard for miles around, as it lies in wait for its prey.

Small children are one of the Kappa's favourite meals, although they will also eat adults.

Water spirits, called Kappas, are said to haunt rivers and ponds in Japan. They are believed to have scaly skin, webbed feet and to be able to swim like fish. The Kelpie is a mythological water horse from Scotland. It lures a human on to its back, then dives into the deepest lake and drowns its unfortunate victim.

In Scandinavian mythology, Kelpies are known as brook horses.

A Bunyip creeping out of a swamp.

Giants

Monsters of enormous size and strength appear in many of the world's myths and legends. The English word for these colossal beings is 'Giant', derived from one of the most famous ancient examples, the Gigantes, of Greek mythology.

The Gigantes

In Ancient Greece, the Gigantes are the giant children of the Gaia, goddess of the Earth, and Uranus, god of the sky. Furious that another group of her children, the Titans, has been imprisoned by the gods of Mount Olympus, Gaia encourages the Gigantes to wage war against the Olympians. The fierce battle that follows is sometimes known as the Gigantomachy.

Led by Alcyoneus and Porphyrion, the Gigantes attempt to reach the top of Mount Olympus by stacking three other mountain ranges on top of each other. Unperturbed, the Olympians call on the hero, Heracles (see page 37) for help. He kills Alcyoneus, then shoots Porphyrion with an arrow, after Zeus has struck him with lightning. Soon the gods' defeat of the Gigantes is complete. The gods once more take control of the world and condemn the Gigantes to the underworld.

Atlas is the leader of the Titans who lost a war with the Olympian gods. Zeus condemns him to stand on the edge of the world and hold up the sky on his shoulders.

An ancient carving from India depicting the goddess Durga doing battle with the Daityas.

Other Warring Giants

In other mythologies, giants are creatures of chaos who are frequently in conflict with the gods. In Hinduism the giants are called Daityas. They fight against the gods, with varying degrees of success. In Norse mythology, the Jotuns, or giants, live in Jotunheim, one of the nine worlds, and often do battle with the gods, even though many are related to them by marriage. It is believed that these battles will become fiercer and, at the final battle of Ragnarok, the Jotuns will storm Asgard and kill most of the gods. Another important Norse giant is Ymir, from whose body the world was created. Odin and his brothers used Ymir's flesh to create the earth. The blood of Ymir formed seas and lakes.

A painting by Marten Eskil Winge (1872) showing the final battle between the giants and the gods.

The giants of Irish mythology were called the Formorians.

Legend says that the Giant's Causeway on the coast of north-east Ireland was built by a giant.

The Formorians

Irish mythology has tales of war-like giants, called the Formorians, who have lived in Ireland since ancient times. It is thought that they represent the forces of chaos and nature, as opposed to the Tuatha De Danaan, a wise race of god-like people who know the art of magic. Legend tells how the Formorians fight off waves of settlers who come to live in Ireland but they are eventually defeated by the Tuatha De Danaan at the second Battle of Magh Tuireadh. The Formorians are led by the giant, Balor, who has an evil eye that kills anything it glances on. In the battle, the hero, Lug, himself half-Formorian, kills Balor, then drives the defeated giants into the sea.

A Jentil building an ancient monument.

Giant stones

In many cultures, legends tell how giants shape the landscape. The frost giants of Norse mythology are said to have carved out the rivers, valleys and fjords. They were born from the sweat of the giant, Ymir (see page 33), the first living being, and lived in Niflheim, the land of ice. The great god, Odin, killed Ymir and used his bones and teeth to make the rocks and mountains. The Giant's Causeway in Northern Ireland was built by the giant, Fionn mac Cumhaill.

In Basque mythology (the Basques are a people from south-west France and north-central Spain), a race of giants called the Jentil, or Jentilak, live alongside humans. They are very hairy, very tall and they can walk across the sea. They are also believed to be so strong that they can hurl huge rocks down from the mountains where they live. This rock-throwing is said to explain the ancient stone monuments and standing stones found in the region.

One-eyed Giants

In Greek mythology, the Cyclops are enormously strong giants, with one eye in the middle of their foreheads. They make the weapons of the gods, and fight for the gods against the Titans. The Cyclops live as shepherds on an island of the same name.

Homer's Odyssey tells the story of the journey home of the hero, Odysseus, after the Trojan War. On his way, Odysseus and his men land on the island of Cyclops where the giant, Polyphemus, imprisons them in his cave and begins to eat them, one by one. To escape, Odysseus uses a stick to blind Polyphemus as he sleeps. When Polyphemus lets his sheep out of his cave, Odysseus and his men cling to the underside of the sheep to make their escape.

A Cyclops tends his flock of sheep.

A Troll rests in a forest.

Trolls

The Trolls of Scandinavian folk and fairytales are enormously strong and ugly creatures who come out of their caves at nighttime to hunt for human prey. Although dressed like human beings, they sometimes have a tail hidden inside their clothing. They are said to be possessed of magical powers which they use to cause mischief and harm. Often invisible, they can also take the shape of animals and trees.

Ogres

Unlike giants, who may be good or bad, Ogres are always cruel and dangerous and are said to feed on human beings. They are first mentioned in fairytales from the 17th century and have since appeared in many works of literature. In art, Ogres are usually shown with immensely strong bodies, large heads, and bushy beards. Ogres often appear in modern literature, films and computer games as villainous and dangerous to humans, but quite easily tricked.

In this painting by Italian artist, Giovanni Lanfanco, a couple are terrorised by a gigantic Ogre.

Rock hurler

The legendary Irish hero, Fionn mac Cumhail (Finn McCool) is also known as a giant. There are many stories about his life and adventures. Among them is the tale of how Fionn and his teacher, Finneces, catch the salmon of knowledge. Fionn accidently eats some of the salmon's skin, which means that he gains all the knowledge in the world. Fionn is also held responsible for carving out many features of the landscape. Legend says that he built the Giant's Causeway (see page 34) as a roadway to Scotland. He is also said to have created the Isle of Man by tearing up part of Ireland and hurling it at a rival. It missed and landed in the sea. The empty space left behind became Lough Neagh.

Fionn mac Cumhail hurled part of Ireland into the Irish Sea, making the Isle of Man. A smaller rock became the island of Rockall.

Talking Heads

Legend says that Bran's head is buried where the Tower of London stands today.

In Welsh mythology, Bran the Blessed is a giant and a great king of Britain. His story is told in an ancient collection of tales, called the Mabinogion. Bran and his army fight the Irish over the mistreatment of Branwen, Bran's sister. The Welsh win the war but only seven of their men survive. They include Bran, who is mortally wounded. He orders his men to cut off his head and bury it in London. His head continues to talk to the men throughout the coming years.

Hero Giants

In Homer's Iliad, the Greek hero and warrior, Ajax, is described as being immensely tall, strong and brave in battle. During the Trojan War, Ajax is chosen to fight the Trojan hero, Hector. Later, he quarrels with Odysseus over Achilles' armour and kills himself in shame.

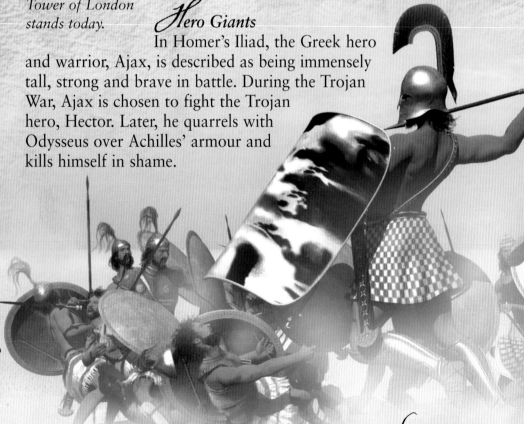

Ajax is the most famous of the Greek warriors. He goes into battle, wielding a huge hammer and bearing a great shield made from seven ox-hides. When Achilles is killed, Ajax uses his hammer to fight off the Trojans so that he and Odysseus can get Achilles' body and take it safely back to their camp for burial.

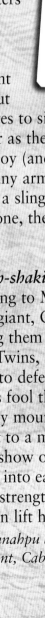

Wrestling Matches

Antaeus, a giant of Greek myth, is the son of the gods, Gaia and Poseidon. As long as he remains in contact with the ground, he will not lose his amazing strength. In order to collect human skulls to build a temple to his father, Antaeus challenges everyone he meets to a wrestling match. Ever the winner, Antaeus then kills his victims. But, legend says, the giant meets his match in the great hero, Heracles. Discovering the secret of Antaeus's power, Heracles uses his cunning to defeat the giant. Unable to beat him by throwing him to the ground, Heracles lifts the giant into the air and crushes him in a bearhug.

Heracles crushing the giant, Antaeus, to death.

Biblical Giants

One of the best-known encounters between a giant and a human appears in the Bible (Book of Samuel). In a battle between the Israelites and the Philistines, the giant Philistine warrior, Goliath, comes out every day and challenges the Israelites to single combat. No one takes up the offer as they are too afraid. Eventually, David, a shepherd boy (and future King of Israel) steps forward. Refusing any armour, David approaches Goliath, armed only with a sling and a few stones. He kills the giant with a stone, then cuts off his head.

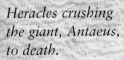

A 19th-century painting showing the battle between David and the giant, Goliath.

Earth-shaking Giants

According to Maya legends, earthquakes are caused by the giant, Cabracan, shaking the mountains by tapping them with his foot. To protect the Earth, the Hero Twins, Hunahpu and Xbalanque, set out on a quest to defeat the giant. Though gods, the Hero Twins fool the giant into thinking that they are simply mountain hunters. They offer to lead the giant to a mountain they had discovered where he can show off his powers. On the way, they trick him into eating a poisoned bird which robs him of his strength. His legs feel so weak that he cannot even lift his feet.

Hunahpu and Xbalanque meet the mountain-shaking giant, Cabracan.

A modern Werewolf transforming from human to wolf

Shapeshifters

An 18th-century German woodcut of a Werewolf shapeshifting.

Almost every culture around the world has myths about shapeshifting. While the popular idea of a shapeshifter is of a human who magically transforms into an animal, there are numerous stories about animals that can also transform themselves.

Werewolves

Throughout northern Europe and North America, legends of Werewolves are told. Arguably, the most famous of the shapeshifters, Werewolves are humans with the ability to transform themselves into ferocious, man-eating wolves. It is said that this transformation takes place at the time of a full moon. A person, usually a man, becomes a Werewolf because another

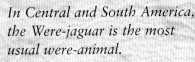

In Central and South America, the Were-jaguar is the most usual were-animal.

Perhaps the most famous Vampire, Count Dracula appeared in the 1897 novel by Bram Stoker.

Werewolf has bitten him or because he has been put under a curse. One way to kill a Werewolf is with a weapon made from silver, such as a bullet or a knife. A Werewolf always shifts back into human shape just before it dies.

Shapeshifters similar to Werewolves are found in many myths. Most of them involve humans transforming into animals other than wolves. In India, for example, tales are told of the Were-tiger, a sorcerer who terrorises livestock and might, at any time, turn to eating people, instead, as its prey.

Vampires

In legends, ancient and modern, Vampires are living corpses who pierce their victims' skin with their terrifying fangs and suck their blood. Vampires are active only at night. As daylight approaches, they must return to the safety of their coffins. They are said to be able to shapeshift between human and bat form.

A Navajo Yeenaaldlooshi is usually shown as naked, except for a coyote or wolf skin.

A Strigoi rises from its grave.

Souls of the dead

In Romanian mythology, Strigoi are evil souls of the dead that rise from their graves at night. They transform into animals or ghosts and haunt the countryside, terrorising anyone they happen to meet. They are said to be closely related to Werewolves (see page 39).

Selkies and Swan Maidens

Some shapeshifters are able to change their form only if they have an article of clothing or a layer of skin. One such creature is the Selkie of Scottish legend. Selkies can transform themselves from seals into humans. To do this, they have to take off their seal skins, then put them back on to turn into animals again. Sometimes humans hide the seal skins, forcing the Selkies to remain in human form. Likewise, the Swan Maidens of Norse legend must wear a magical robe of swan feathers in order to shapeshift from humans into swans.

Swan Maidens bathing, having taken off their swan robes.

A Selkie reaches for her seal skin.

40

Skinwalkers and Berserkers

Some Native American myths tell of shapeshifting Skinwalkers, humans who are able to transform themselves into any animal they wish. One of the best-known Skinwalkers is the Yeenaaldlooshii of Navajo legend. It is most commonly seen as a wolf, coyote, owl, crow or fox. Skinwalkers are greatly feared because they attack humans and can steal a person's skin, or soul, by staring into a person's eyes.

In Norse legend, assuming an animal's shape also means assuming its character. A famous example are the Berserkers, warriors who wear bear skins, and fight with the strength and ferocity of a bear. Other warriors, called Ulfhednar, or 'wolf-coats', wear wolf skins on their heads when they go into battle. Like the Berserkers, they are famous for the ferociousness of their fighting.

Many-tailed Foxes

Fox-like creatures appear often in Japanese mythology. They are known as Kitsune, and are said to be wise and intelligent. The more tails a Kitsune has, the wiser it is said to be. Kitsune also possess magical powers. Among these is the ability to change shape and transform themselves into humans.

Egyptian gods, Horus and Seth

A 19th-century print, showing the Japanese Prince Hanzoku being tormented by a Kitsune.

Shapeshifting Gods

In various mythology, deities use their power to change shape. Egyptian myths tell how the god, Seth, changes into a pig, then a hippo before being defeated by Horus. In Greek legend, Zeus shapeshifts on several occasions to win the attention of mortal women. He appears to Europa as a white bull, to Leda as a swan, and to Danae as a shower of gold.

Europa is carried off by Zeus, disguised as a white bull.

A demon bursts from the depths of Hell.

Demons, Ghouls & Ghosts

Creatures that represent evil and darkness are an important concept in many religions, cultures and folklores. The opposite of goodness and purity, demons and ghouls bring terror to people, while witches are often considered malevolent.

Demons come in many forms, such as Buer, the demon leader, who is shown here with a lion's head and five goats' legs surrounding his body.

Demons

Demons are a fundamental part of many religions in which their appearances are remarkably similar and generally malevolent. They are often found in opposition to the gods, God, or forces of good. In Hindu mythology, demons are evil beings called Rakshasas, that are in constant battle against the gods. In Christianity, demons are considered to be angels who fell from favour by rebelling against God. They are the cause of evil and ignorance in the world. Their leader is commonly known as the Devil, or Satan. In Japanese folklore, Oni are gigantic demons with sharp claws, fangs and two horns growing out of their heads. They are often shown carrying a club and dressed in tiger skin. Their skin is usually red or blue in colour. Oni may originally have been evil spirits who caused disease and disaster. In some parts of Japan, festivals were held each year to drive the Oni away. More recently, the Oni have been given a more protective role and are themselves believed to ward off bad luck.

In different cultures, the Devil has different names, including Abbadon, Angra Mainyu, Satan, Asmodai, Beelzebub, Lucifer, Belias and Iblis.

A ferocious-looking Rakshasa appears in a temple painting (above). A statue of an Oni, brandishing a club (below).

Gargoyles and Grotesques

A Gargoyle is a stone carving which decorates cathedrals and churches, and has a spout for carrying rain water away. A Grotesque is similar but does not function as a waterspout. Gargoyles often show monsters or demon-like creatures. They are believed to protect the building from evil spirits.

One of the many Gargoyles which look down from Notre Dame Cathedral in Paris, France.

Ghoul

In ancient Arabian legends, a ghoul, or gul, is a monstrous demon that can take the shape of an animal, especially a dog or hyena. It lives in the desert and lures travellers into its den where it kills and eats them. It also haunts graveyards where it opens graves and feasts on the dead. In European literature, ghouls live among the undead, alongside zombies (see below). Once human, these hideous creatures live off human flesh and cannot tolerate sunlight. Traditionally, it is said, ghouls could be driven away by ringing the church bells.

A ghoul raids a desert graveyard.

Zombies are popular in modern horror films.

Djinn

In the religion of Islam, Djinn are invisible beings created by Allah (God) from fire. They can be either good or evil, having the same free will as human beings. They are thought to live in places that are unclean, and to cause fear and confusion when they meddle in human affairs. Sometimes, they attempt to take over human bodies. The chief of the Djinns is Shaitan, or Iblis. He disobeys Allah and becomes the enemy of humans, seeking to turn them away from Allah.

Fantastical Djinns, or Genies, are also found in folk tales from Arabia, Persia and India, most notably in The Arabian Nights. In the story of Aladdin, a Djinn is imprisoned in an old brass lamp. The Djinn obeys whoever rubs the lamp and sets it free.

Zombies

Zombies are corpses that have been brought back to life. They originated on the island of Haiti where they play an important part in Voodoo beliefs. It is said that they are revived by a sorcerer and remain under his control because they have no free will of their own. In modern horror films, Zombies are usually shown as robotic, flesh-eating creatures whose bodies have begun to decompose. They often travel in large groups, or mobs.

A Djinn is made from fire and can take any form it chooses.

Hags, Witches and Banshees

Hags are generally depicted as wizened old women and appear in myths and folk tales from around the world. The word 'hag' may come from an old English word for witch. Though sometimes viewed as good and fairy-like, Hags are often considered malevolent, bringing nightmares (see below), and frightening children. One famous and hideous Hag is Baba Yaga who appears in many Eastern European myths. She is said to fly around in a giant mortar (a bowl used for grinding spices and herbs), using a pestle (grinder) as a paddle. She lives deep in the forest in a log cabin that stands on chicken's legs, surrounded by a fence of spikes, each with a human skull on top. Most stories tell how she kidnaps children, her favourite food, and brings about storms and tempests. A few stories tell a different tale, however, of how Baba Yaga helps people who are lost or on a quest.

In Irish mythology, a Banshee is a female spirit, or fairy, who is seen as a bringer of death. Her wailing voice can be heard if someone is about to die. Some families, especially noble ones, were said to have Banshees attached to them. Banshees are often described as wearing white or grey, with long, fair hair.

A painting of Baba Yaga

A Banshee may wail softly for a peaceful death; more loudly for a violent one.

The three witches from Shakespeare's Macbeth, illustrated by Arthur Rackham.

The stuff of Nightmares

A Mara, or Mare, is a female demon from Scandinavian mythology. Mares are said to move about at night, entering rooms through keyholes or under the door. They crouch on a sleeper's chest, causing bad dreams, hence the name - nightmares.

The Nightmare, painted by Henry Fuseli in 1781.

Glossary

Aboriginal
Referring to the Aborigines, the original inhabitants of Australia who arrived there thousands of years ago.

Arthurian
Stories relating to the time of King Arthur, a legendary British king.

Beneficial
Something good and positive.

Benevolent
Helpful, friendly or kindly.

Caiman
A reptile related to alligators and crocodiles.

Coyote
A dog-like animal that lives in the deserts and prairies of North America.

Deity
Another word for a god or a goddess.

Extinct
A plant or animal, real or mythical, that has died out and can never exist again.

Fjords
Long, narrow inlets of the sea which run between steep, high cliffs, commonly found in Norway.

Folklore
The traditional stories and legends of a people or culture that sum up their beliefs and often describe events that happened in their past.

Heraldic
Relating to heraldry. Heraldry is the symbolic images, decorations and colours used to represent a ruler, or an important person or family. Heraldic symbols were originally used on armour, flags and shields.

Hero
In Greek mythology, a hero was a being of amazing courage and strength who was often half-mortal, half-god.

Hoards
Large collections or stores of something, such as a dragon's treasure.

Icon
A Christian religious picture, painted on wood and displayed in some Christian churches.

Iliad
A great Ancient Greek poem, said to have been composed by Homer in the 8th or 9th centuries BC. The work is based on the legend of the Trojan War.

Immortality
Never dying but living for ever.

Invulnerable
Not able to be wounded or hurt.

Legends
Traditional stories which are often based on supposedly historical events. Like myths, legends were originally passed down by word of mouth by storytellers.

Malevolent
Wishing evil on others; another word for malicious.

Manatees
Large, air-breathing sea mammals, sometimes called sea cows. Sailors may have mistaken them for mermaids.

Maritime
Relating to the sea.

Millennia
A millennium (singular) is a thousand years.

Medieval
Relating to the Middle Ages, a period of European history which lasted from around the 5th century to the 15th century AD.

Myths
Traditional stories, not based in historical fact but using supernatural characters to explain human behaviour and natural events. Myths helped ancient people to understand the world around them.

Nymph
In Greek mythology, a nymph was a spirit of nature who appeared as a beautiful girl.

Odyssey
A great Ancient Greek poem, said to have been composed by Homer, in the 8th or 9th centuries BC. It tells of the adventures of the hero, Odysseus, as he returned from the Trojan War.

Quest
In medieval legends, an expedition by a knight or group of knights to accomplish a task, such as the search for a mythical beast.

Quetzal
A bird from tropical Central America which has beautiful red and green plumage. Its feathers were highly prized by the Aztecs and other peoples of the region.

Sacrifices
When humans or animals are killed and offered to the gods or goddesses in order to win their favour.

Sorcerer
A person who uses magical powers. Another word for a witch or a wizard.

Strait
A narrow channel of sea water.

Supernatural
Magical beings, such as fairies, ghosts and gods, and events that cannot be explained by physical or scientific laws.

Torso
The trunk, or top part, of a human body.

Voodoo
A religion which is practised mainly on the Caribbean island of Haiti.

Index

Ahuizotl, 17
Ajax, 36
Alphyn, 19
Ammit, 18
Angels, 15
Antaeus, 37
Apep, 8
Aspidochelone, 29

Baba Yaga, 45
Baku, 20
Banshees, 45
Basilisk, 17, 21
Bastet, 25
Bicorne, 26
Bran the Blessed, 36
Bunyips, 31
Buraq, 11

Cabracan, 37
Cadmus, Prince, 7
Calygreyhound, 19
Catoblepas, 21
Centaurs, 25, 27, 36
Charybdis, 30
Chichevache, 26
Chimera, 11, 17-21
Cockatrice, 17
Cyclops, 35
Cynocephalus, 25

Daityas, 33
Demons, 42, 43
Djinn, 44
Dragons, 6, 7
Dragon slayers, 6, 7

El hombre caiman
    ('Caiman man'), 26
Enfield, 19
Eros (Cupid), 14

Fafnir, 7
Fauns (Satyrs), 24
Fionn mac Cumhail, 36

Firebird, 13
Formorians, 34

Ganesha, 25
Gargoyles, 43
Garuda, 14, 24
George, St, 7
Ghouls, 44
Giants, 32-37
Gigantes, 33
Goliath, 37
Gorgons, 26
Griffin, 11
Grotesques, 43

Hags, 45
Harpies, 12
Heracles, 9, 33, 37
Hermes (Mercury), 14
Hippocampus, 30
Hippogriff, 10, 11
Horus, 41
Hsigo (Hsaio), 12
Hydra 9

Ipotane, 24

Jengu, 27
Jentil (Jentilak), 34
Jormungandr, 9, 29
Jotuns, 33

Kappas, 31
Kelpies, 31
Kirin, 20
Kitsune, 41
Kraken, 29

Lake monsters, 31
Lamassu (see Shedu), 12
Leviathan, 29
Leyaks, 15
Lindworms, 8

Manticore, 21

Mara, 45
Medusa, 26
Melusine, 27
Mere Folk, 27
Mermaids, 27
Mermecolion, 18
Merrow, 27
Minotaur, 25

Nagas, 24
Nuckelavee
Nue, 17

Odysseus, 12, 29, 35
Ogres, 35
Oni, 43

Pegasus, 11, 26
Peng, 13
Peryton, 9
Phoenix, 13

Qilin, 20
Questing Beast, 19
Quetzalcoatl, 8

Rakshasas, 43
Roc 13
Rompo, 18
Rusalka, 27

Satyrs (Fauns), 24
Scylla, 30
Sea serpents, 29
Selkies, 27, 40
Serpopards, 18
Seth, 41
Shapeshifters, 38-41
Shedu (see Lamassu), 12
Siegfried, 7
Simurgh, 11
Sirens, 12
Sirins, 12
Skinwalkers 40, 41
Sobek, 25

Sphinxes, 18
Strigoi, 40
Swan Maidens, 40

Tarasque, 21
Tengu, 15
Thunderbird, 13
Trolls, 35

Unicorns, 20
Ushi-oni, 21

Vampires, 39
Vucub-Cacquix, 13

Werewolves, 39
Worms, 8
Wyverns, 8

Yeenaaldlooshii, 40, 41
Ymir, 33, 34

Zeus, 41
Ziz, 13
Zombies, 44